Diplodocus

by Grace Hansen

abdopublishing.com

Published by Abdo Kids, a division of ABDO, P.O. Box 398166, Minneapolis, Minnesota 55439.

Copyright © 2018 by Abdo Consulting Group, Inc. International copyrights reserved in all countries. No part of this book may be reproduced in any form without written permission from the publisher.

Printed in the United States of America, North Mankato, Minnesota.

052017

092017

 THIS BOOK CONTAINS RECYCLED MATERIALS

Photo Credits: Alamy, AP Images, Depositphotos Enterprise, iStock, Science Source, Shutterstock, Thinkstock

Production Contributors: Teddy Borth, Jennie Forsberg, Grace Hansen

Design Contributors: Dorothy Toth, Laura Mitchell

Publisher's Cataloging in Publication Data

Names: Hansen, Grace, author.

Title: Diplodocus / by Grace Hansen.

Description: Minneapolis, Minnesota : Abdo Kids, 2018 | Series: Dinosaurs |
    Includes bibliographical references and index.

Identifiers: LCCN 2016962375 | ISBN 9781532100376 (lib. bdg.) |
    ISBN 9781532101069 (ebook) | ISBN 9781532101618 (Read-to-me ebook)

Subjects: LCSH: Diplodocus--Juvenile literature. | Dinosaurs--North America--
    Juvenile literature.

Classification: DDC 567.913--dc23

LC record available at http://lccn.loc.gov/2016962375

Table of Contents

Diplodocus

Diplodocus lived during the late **Jurassic period**, around 150 million years ago.

Diplodocus were **sauropods**. Sauropods were large plant eaters.

Habitat

Diplodocus lived in grasslands on the edges of forests. Rivers and lakes were nearby.

Body

A Diplodocus weighed more than 20,000 pounds (9,072 kg). It could grow more than 80 feet (24.4 m) long.

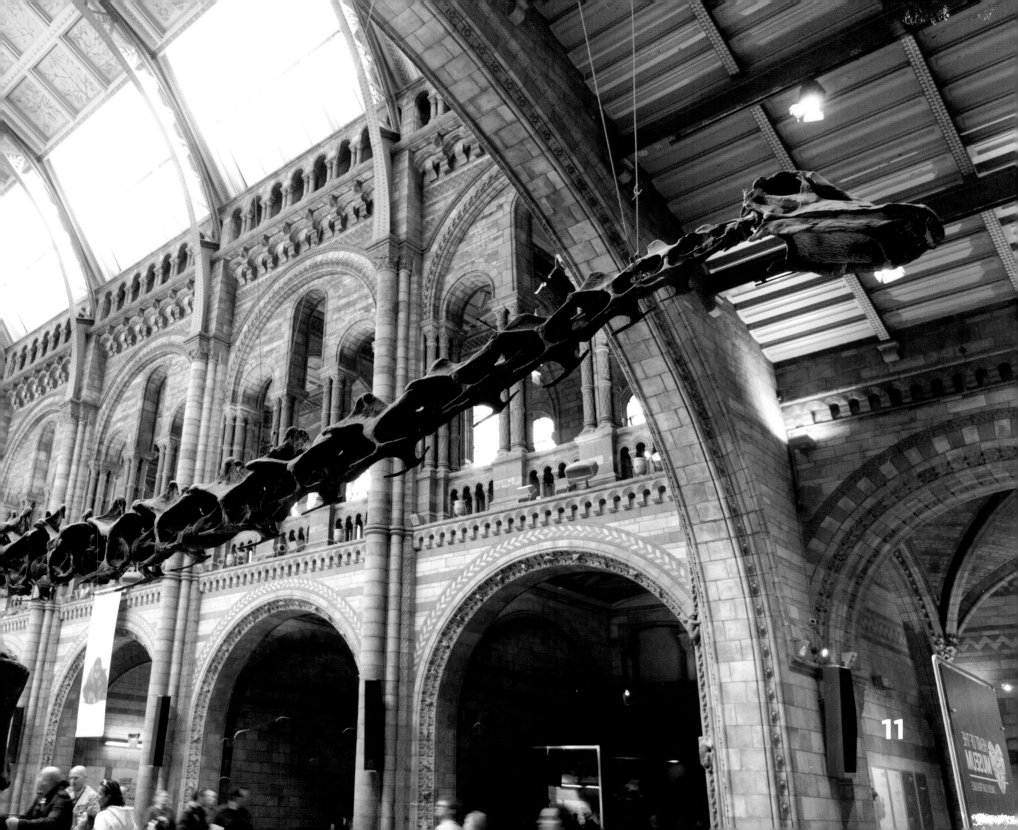

Its head, neck, and tail made up about 80% of its length. Four strong legs supported this dinosaur's very long body.

60%

20%

100%

13

Its head was small in comparison to the dinosaur's body. The mouth held 40 peg-shaped teeth. Its teeth tilted forward just a bit.

Food

Diplodocus ate plants. They stripped branches of their leaves. They had to eat a lot due to their huge size.

Diplodocus probably held their heads low. They may have reared onto their back legs to eat from treetops. But it was likely easier for them to eat from low plants.

19

Fossils

The first Diplodocus **fossils** were found in 1877. They were uncovered in Morrison, Colorado. Since then, many more remains have been found.

Colorado

More Facts

- **Fossil** hunters Earl Douglas and Samuel W. Williston were the first to uncover Diplodocus fossils in 1877.

- Othniel C. Marsh, a fossil scientist, named Diplodocus in 1878. He used the Greek words "diplos" (meaning "double") and "dokos" (meaning "beam").

- A Diplodocus may have fought other dinosaurs with its tail, which it could use like a whip.

Glossary

fossils – the remains, impression, or trace of something that lived long ago, as a skeleton, footprint, etc.

Jurassic period – named after the Jura Mountains where rocks of this age were first found, this time period saw many lush plants, large plant-eating dinosaurs, and smaller meat-eating dinosaurs.

sauropod – a very large plant-eating dinosaur that stood on four long legs and had a long neck and tail, and a small head.

Index

abdokids.com

Use this code to log on to abdokids.com and access crafts, games, videos and more!

Abdo Kids Code:
DDK0376